Basher Science™ MINI

PANDEMIC

KINGFISHER
LONDON & NEW YORK

KINGFISHER
LONDON & NEW YORK

www.basherscience.com

First published 2021 in the United States by Kingfisher
120 Broadway, New York, NY 10271
Kingfisher is an imprint of Macmillan Children's Books, London

Author: Tom Jackson
Consultant: Dr. Elizabeth Wortley
Editor: Anna Southgate
Designer: Dave Jones
Proofreader: Richard Beatty

Distributed in the U.S. and Canada by Macmillan,
120 Broadway, New York, NY 10271

Library of Congress Cataloging-in-Publication Data has been applied for.

ISBN: 978-0-7534-7786-1 (Hardcover)
ISBN: 978-0-7534-7787-8 (Paperback)

Printed in China
9 8 7 6 5 4 3 2 1
1TR/0221/WKT/RV/128MA

CONTENTS

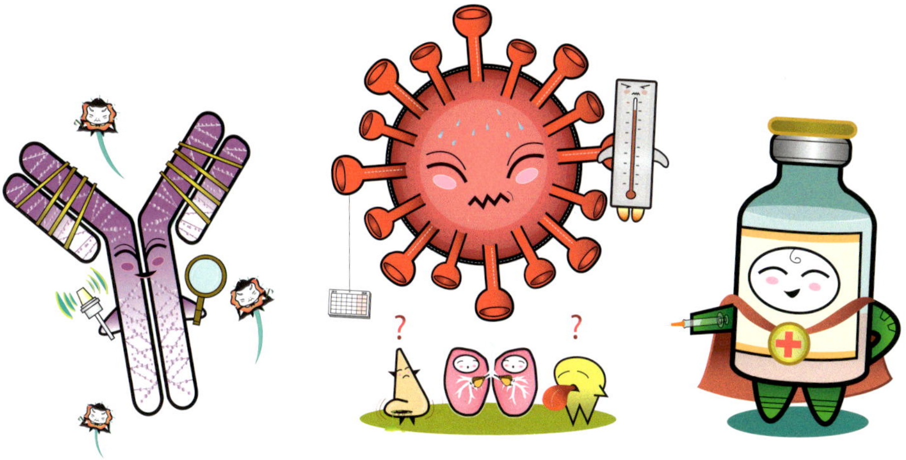

Introduction

Pandemic

Infections are a natural part of life—we've all had one. Most, such as a cold or chicken pox, are not life-threatening. Sometimes a doctor gives us medicine to make us better. But sadly, now and then, an infection wins and a person dies. Medical experts explore ways to beat infections, and part of the fight is learning how they spread. One thing infections can do is surge up in a sudden outbreak, or epidemic, where many people get sick all at once. If the infection causing an epidemic is new, as with The Plague in the 1300s and COVID-19 in 2020, it can spread rapidly around the world to become a pandemic.

The battle to control pandemics began with a doctor in London, England, named John Snow. In the 1850s, he saved thousands of lives by tracking the victims of a cholera outbreak and tracing the cause of the deadly disease. Snow found that victims were drinking dirty water drawn from a single city pump. He sealed off the supply, and the cholera went away! This smart work was the start of public health medicine, which is still fighting hard to keep us all safe from pandemics. Come and find out how it works.

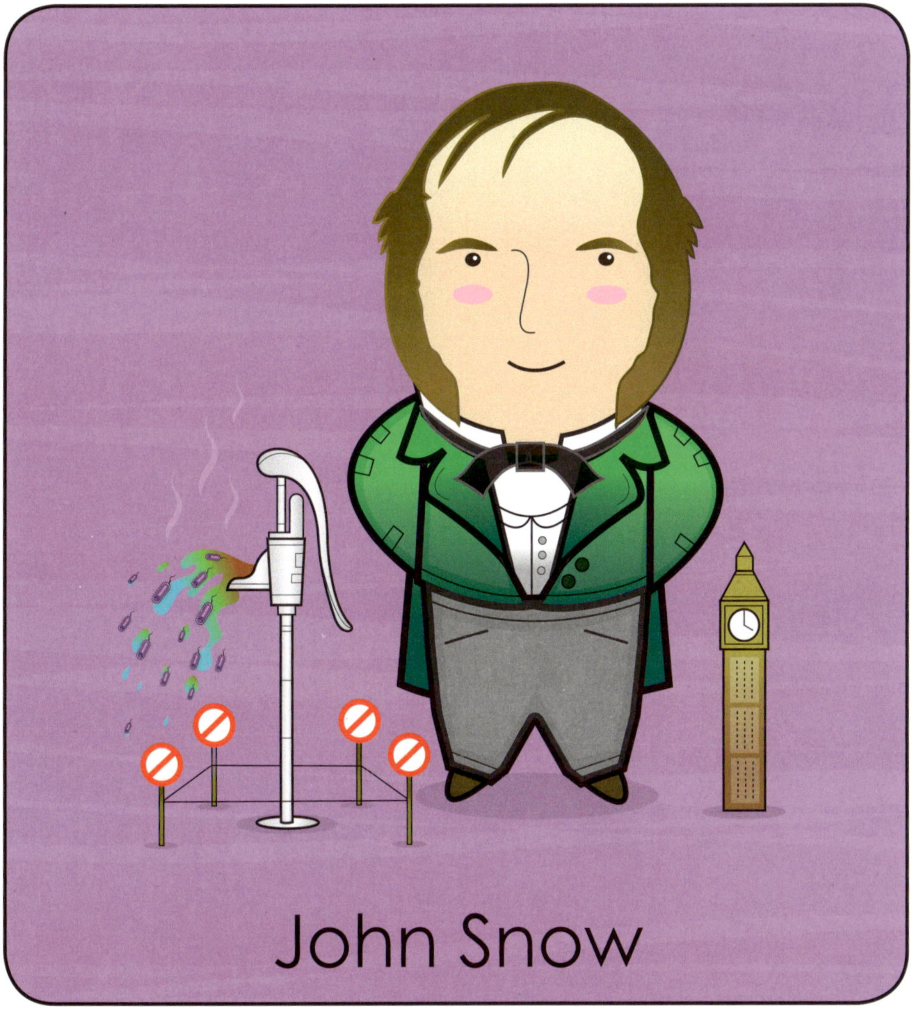
John Snow

Chapter 1
Infectious Invaders

We cause diseases, and we're very good at it. Boo, hiss to you, too! Keep your sneers and taunts to yourself. Save your energy for finding out more about us. Know your enemy, they say, and it will help you fight back. We are history's biggest pandemic diseases—vicious types such as The Plague and HIV. Each of us is unique, but we all have our weaknesses. Find those and you just might be able to land a knockout blow with a cure. It's true, we invaders have lost every battle waged so far, but not without a nasty brawl. And look who's here now—COVID-19, the latest player on our team. Ready for another fight?

The Plague

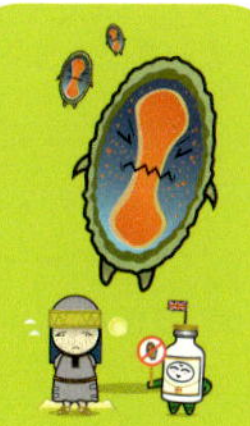

Smallpox

Cholera

Spanish Flu

HIV

Ebola

Virus

Coronavirus

COVID-19

The Plague

Infectious Invaders

- A beastly disease spread by flea bites
- Symptoms include swollen glands and internal bleeding
- Killed more than 75 million in history's biggest pandemic ever

AKA the Black Death, I'm Poppa Pandemic, the Big Daddy of disease. In the 1300s, I killed half the population of Europe and Asia in just four years!

I'm caused by bacteria in fleas, mostly the type that live on rats. In the past, every ship on the seven seas had stowaway rats aboard, and they spread my germs at every port. In the 1300s, it seems fleas infected so many rats that the rodents died in huge numbers. Running out of living bodies to inhabit, the little bugs got hopping mad and found new ones to nibble on—including those of humans. My bacteria get into the blood, and there you have me. I cause aches and pains and a sudden high fever. People developing painful swellings in the armpits and neck may die within days . . . I'm truly horrid, for sure.

- As well as rats, plague is carried by the fleas of prairie dogs and some squirrels
- The Great Fire of London, England, stopped a plague outbreak in the city in 1666
- Powerful medicines can beat the plague nowadays, and outbreaks are rare

The Plague

Smallpox

Infectious Invaders

- A powerful disease that killed one-third of its victims
- Marked survivors with nasty scars known as pockmarks
- Wiped out for good through worldwide vaccination

Small by nature but huge in impact, I was a disease that gave sufferers little pimples (and terrible aches and fevers, too). I used those spots to get around. They swelled with yucky Virus-packed pus, fit to burst. Any seepage got onto fingers, infecting all they touched. Sadly (for me), I was the target of history's first vaccine and was eradicated in 1977. I *won't* be back!

- One of smallpox's earliest known victims was Egyptian Pharaoh Ramses V
- Edward Jenner, an English doctor, created the first smallpox vaccine in 1796
- Smallpox was also known as "speckled monster" and the "red plague"

Cholera

Infectious Invaders

- An ancient disease that spread widely from the 1800s
- It spreads when sewage mixes with drinking water and food
- This stomach-twister can kill in a matter of hours

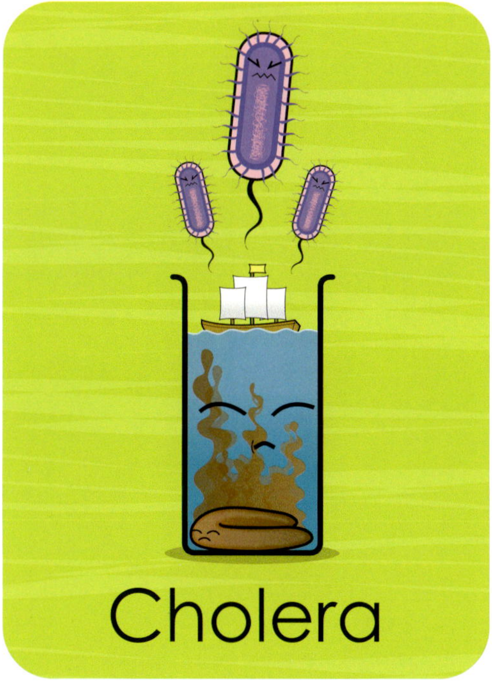

Bottoms up, people! I'm caused by a bacterium that gets into you through dirty water. Once inside the stomach, I pull the flush to cause awful diarrhea that empties the body of water and nutrients. I really took hold when people began living in crowded cities, and I'm the one who got John Snow to study epidemics in the 1850s. Thank me later, I'm still busy infecting four million people a year!

- There were six cholera pandemics between 1817 and 1961
- Ships with cholera onboard used to fly a yellow warning flag and couldn't dock
- John Snow tackled cholera when he pioneered epidemiology in 1854

Spanish Flu

Infectious Invaders

- The top-ranked influenza (AKA flu) outbreak ever
- Causing 50 million deaths, it is one of history's biggest killers
- Damage caused by WWI made it spread and kill quickly

"It's just the flu!" Sound familiar? Well, don't be fooled. Flu is a serious disease that lays people low for days. It can kill, too, especially babies and old people.

I'm history's deadliest flu. I struck in 1918, infecting one-third of the world in two years. Many of my victims were young and healthy. I arrived during World War I and spread among soldiers, first in the U.S. and then France. They tried to keep me hush-hush, but Spain was not involved in the war and stories about me spread from there—I've been called Spanish ever since. I was deadly because I made sufferers so weak they caught other infections, such as pneumonia, which they couldn't fight. In the end, Face Mask and Social Distancing helped beat me. Sure, I'm long gone now, but it's just a matter of time before a cousin of mine breaks out.

- Spanish flu killed three times as many people as World War I (1914–18)
- A theory at the time said the flu was a gas rising from graves of the war dead
- A mutated version of the virus caused the less deadly swine flu pandemic (2009)

Spanish Flu

HIV

Infectious Invaders

- A silent spreader that wipes out the body's disease defenses
- Since appearing in 1981, it has caused 32 million deaths
- Spreads through unprotected sex and infected blood/breast milk

I'm a trickster virus. I sneak inside T Cell to hide from Immune System. Then I tear down the body's defenses against diseases, leaving AIDS in my wake. The body can no longer fight off infections, so even simple bugs such as colds can be deadly. Today, Test and Trace are working hard to slow my infection rate down, while Treatment stops me right in my tracks.

- Treatment inactivates HIV; the person stays healthy and can't pass it on
- AIDS is a late stage of infection when a series of life-threatening illnesses develop
- About 700,000 people die from AIDS every year

Ebola

Infectious Invaders

- A disease that causes internal bleeding under the skin
- Enters through soft tissues in the eyes, nose, and mouth
- Without medical help, up to 90 percent of sufferers die

I'm hideous, a disease that makes people bleed to death on the inside and out. You can catch me just by having infected blood touch your skin. I used to kill nine out of ten of my victims, but Treatment has reduced that by half, and Vaccine is now on the scene. My most recent stomping ground, the Democratic Republic of Congo, was declared epidemic-free in 2020.

- Ebola is highly contagious; caregivers must wear full protective clothing
- Its name comes from Congo's Ebola River, where it was first diagnosed in 1976
- The biggest outbreak killed 11,000 in Sierra Leone, Liberia, and Guinea (2014–16)

Virus

Infectious Invaders

- A DNA devil that causes a wide range of diseases
- This itsy-bitsy attacker hijacks cells to make copies of itself
- Has a coat of protein and fat to protect its crafty DNA code

A secret agent of infection, I create dozens of diseases, from winter colds and chicken pox to Ebola and COVID-19. I'm so small that only the most powerful microscopes can see me, and that makes me hard to fight.

I'm a simple little critter made of a strip of DNA or RNA coiled up inside a slick wrapper of protein and fats. I use a spike protein sticking out of my coat to unlock your defenses and slip inside a cell. My DNA is the same as the stuff that carries your genetic code. It's mission is to hijack your DNA and take over its gene-copying system. Really, all I want is to make more of me . . . millions more, in fact. It's not my intention to hurt you, but your cells become overwhelmed and die, and that's what makes you sick. Sorry, but I have no choice. I just do what I gotta do.

- DNA stands for deoxyribonucleic acid
- RNA (ribonucleic acid) is used by a cell to transport genetic codes
- Viruses often enter through the soft, damp lining of the nose, throat, mouth, eyes

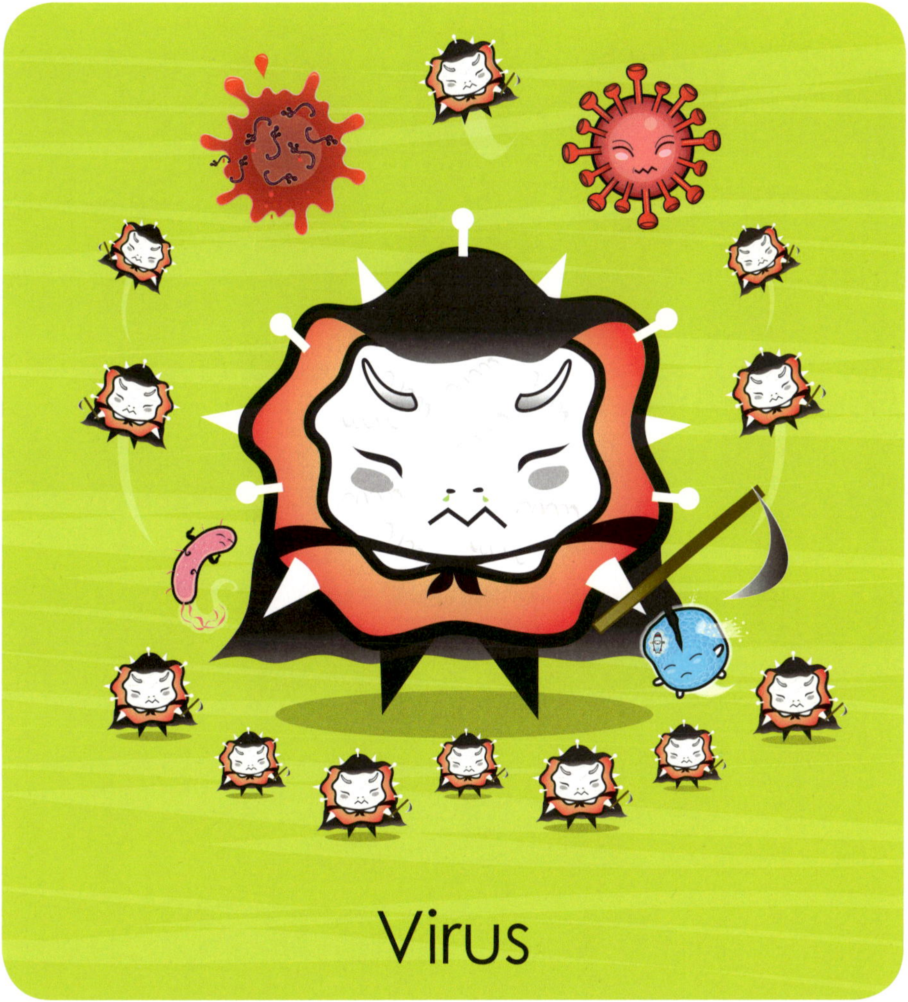
Virus

Coronavirus

Infectious Invaders

- A spiky virus with a big reputation
- Known for causing serious breathing problems
- The virus type behind the COVID-19 pandemic

All rise for King Virus. My name means "crown virus," and under the microscope my coating of pointy proteins looks like a halo of spikes—my crown. I carry RNA, not DNA, and I cause diseases that attack the respiratory system (that's breathing, to you). Your next common cold could be thanks to me, although other kinds of viruses cause colds, too.

I'm more famous for deadly diseases such as SARS (severe acute respiratory syndrome), which appeared in 2002. Spreading easily through the air in coughed-up specks of spit, SARS killed 10 percent of its victims. Public Health Agency halted it, but a new version appeared in 2019. Less deadly, yes, but still a killer, it slipped out of control, spreading around the world in months. And its name? COVID-19, of course. Sorry, guys, that's my bad.

- Coronaviruses that attack humans were discovered in the 1960s
- The SARS outbreak in China and Southeast Asia killed around 770 people
- Deadlier MERS (Middle East respiratory syndrome) kills 35 percent of victims

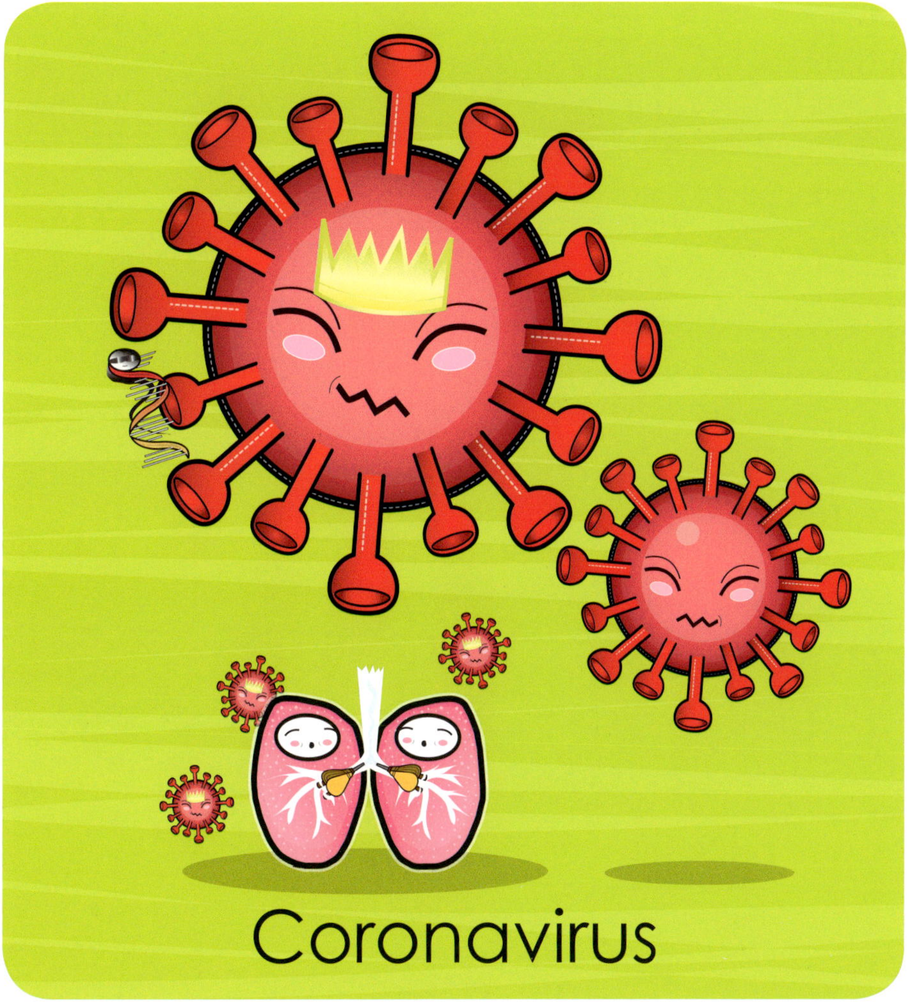

Coronavirus

COVID-19

Infectious Invaders

- A nasty new disease that appeared in 2019
- Older people are most at risk of serious illness
- Symptoms include fever, cough, and a loss of smell and taste

Want my advice? Keep your distance! First recorded in China in December 2019, a year later I had circled the globe and was infecting half a million people a day. Because I was new, I was able to infect the whole world at the same time. That's the very definition of "pandemic."

I'm caused by a coronavirus. Many of my victims get a cough and have breathing problems, but some also have a fever or diarrhea or lose their senses of taste and smell. I'm spread inside the droplets that a person breathes out, especially when coughing. Although most people recover from the disease, my long-term effects remain unknown. Certainly the elderly and those with other diseases risk becoming very sick or dying. Work together to keep everyone protected, and you'll beat me in the end.

- COVID stands for **co**rona**vi**rus **d**isease
- Unless they isolate, the average COVID sufferer passes the disease to three others
- In April 2020, half the world's population was in lockdown to stop it from spreading

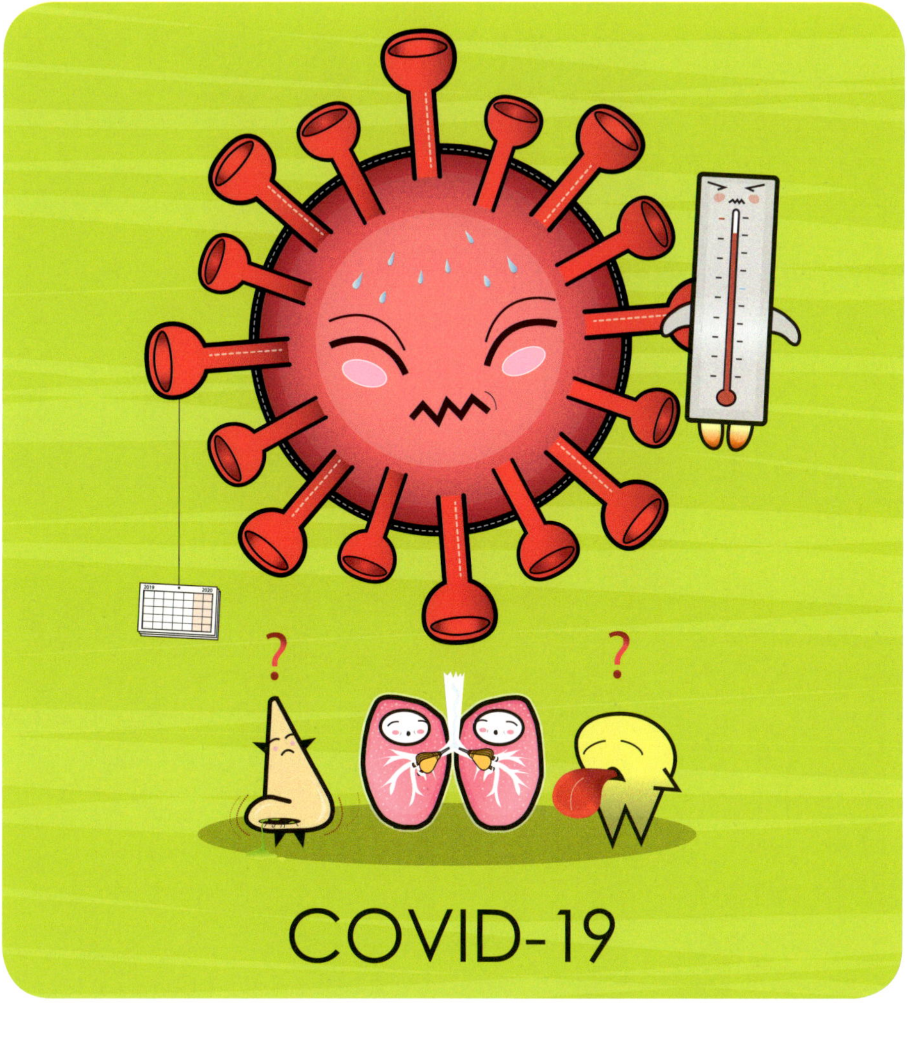
2019
2020
COVID-19

Chapter 2
Virus Busters

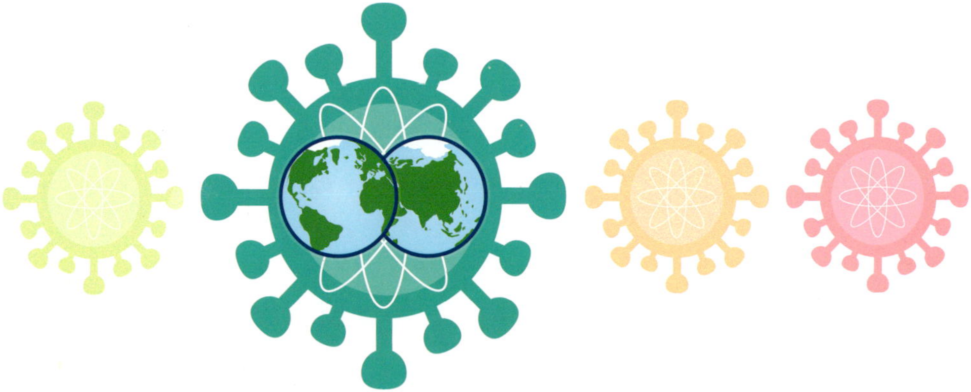

Listen up, people, this is a real emergency—first responders are on their way. We are the Virus Busters, a mixed-up crew of battlers that include your own body system, scientific snoopers who track the attackers, and medical miracles that set out to block a disease's advance. We combine our efforts to give you every chance of survival during a pandemic. Back-room experts Epidemiology and Clinical Trial constantly improve the defenses, while Immune System works with Vaccine to beat back attacks. We Virus Busters have had our successes in the past, and we will never back down.

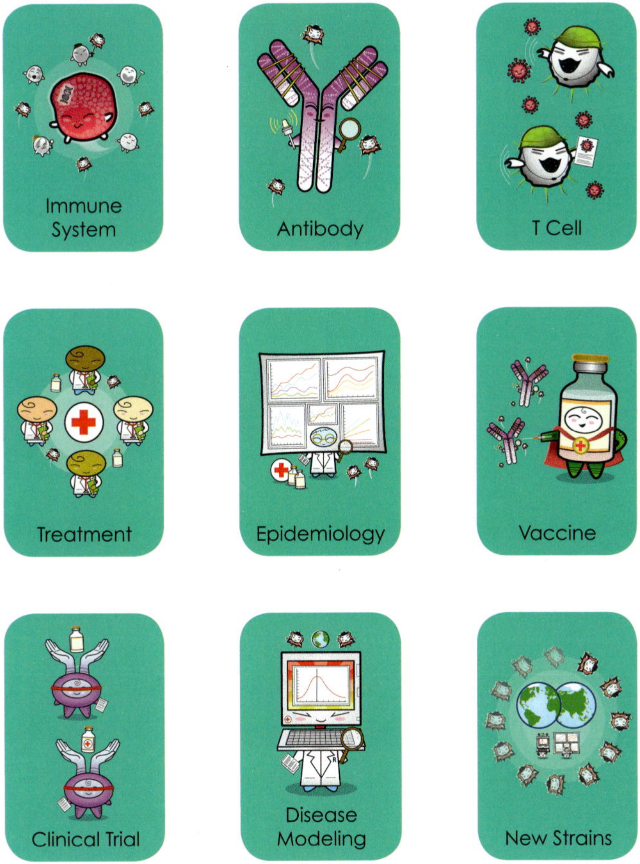
Immune System
Antibody
T Cell
Treatment
Epidemiology
Vaccine
Clinical Trial
Disease Modeling
New Strains

Immune System

Virus Busters

- The body system that's got your back, front, top, and bottom
- A crack team of seek-and-destroy white blood cells
- Boosts body temperature to get the job done ASAP

If your body comes under attack, I'll be your champion, fighting back on your behalf. Me and my army of specialist soldiers, the white blood cells, that is. On alert around your body, these troopers swarm to the front line when Virus attacks, crowding into infected tissues, making them swell and redden. (If your nose runs, that's the team washing out infecting agents in sticky snot. Eew!)

It takes a day or so to get things going, but this is a complex operation! I have garbage guzzlers on my killer team. They swallow attackers and use chemical knives to slice them to smithereens. There are smart coding experts, too—specialists who search for markers (called antigens) that make attackers unique. Once that information comes my way, I clear out the invaders for good—and out they stay!

- The scientific name for a white blood cell is leukocyte
- There are about 3,300 white blood cells in every millionth of a pint of blood
- The brain has an immune system of its own, separate from that of the body

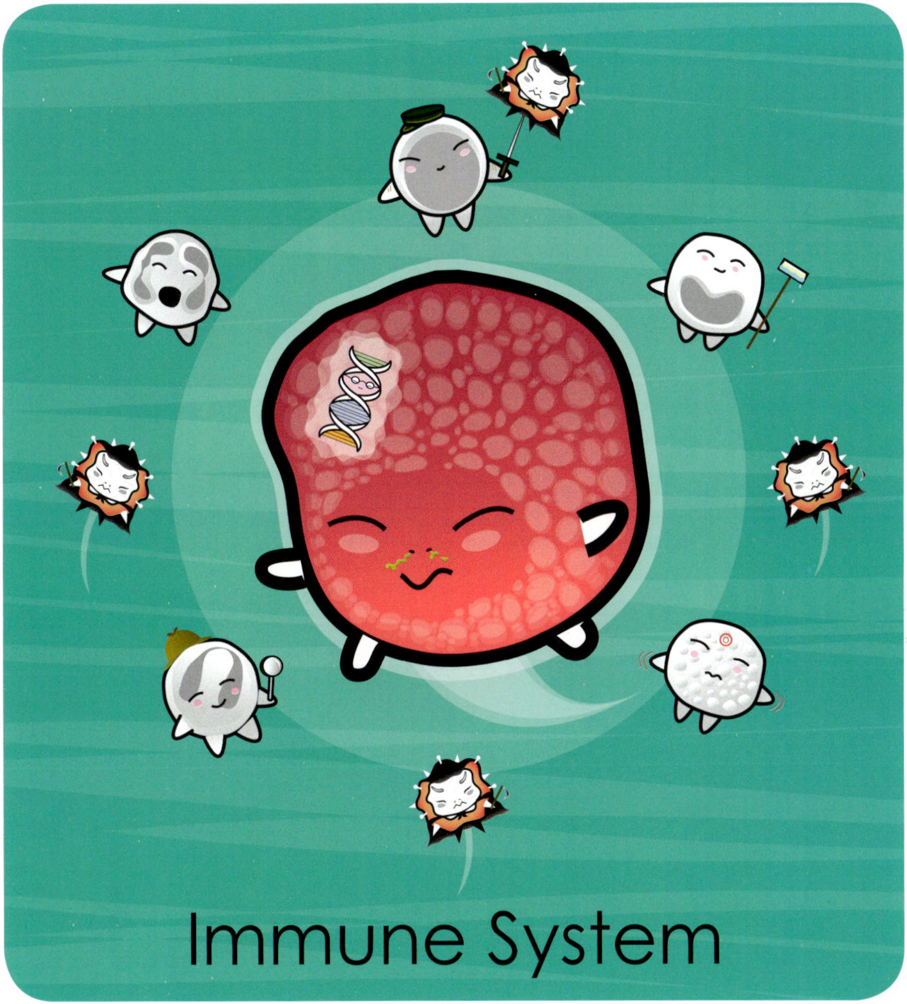
Immune System

Antibody

Virus Busters

- Disease hunter that seeks out infections
- Tooled up to be a perfect fit with a particular bug
- Marks out viruses for destruction to end an illness

Very much pro-body, I help Immune System fight disease. Once an antigen (marker) is found, I mold my Y-shaped body around it so we fit like a key in a lock. Then I multiply by the million, spilling into the blood. I test every chemical I find—if it fits, I've found an attacker! Now I'm a beacon, clustering into blobs that bring in Immune System's destruction crew to finish the job.

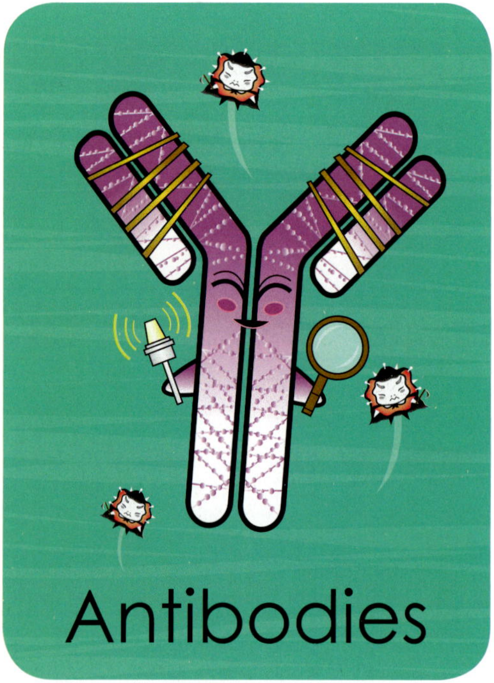

- Antibodies are made from proteins called immunoglobulins
- Plasma cells can release up to 2,000 antibodies a second
- The average antibody is 400 billionths of an inch (10 billionths of a meter) long.

T Cell

Virus Busters

- Tip-top commander and controller of the immune system
- Memory T cells keep a record of past infections
- "T" stands for thymus, which is where the cells are made

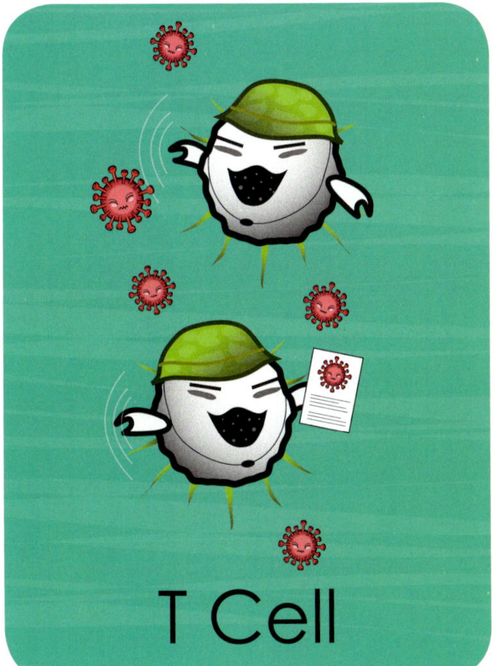

"T" is for tough, tenacious, talented. I'm the type of white blood cell that takes control when an invader attacks. I start up the inflammation and fever that the body needs when it's fighting an infection. Next I organize the production of Antibody and send in the cleanup squad—I can even do the killing myself. Oh, and then I take note of the attacker's info. If it comes back, I'll attack.

- The immune system also uses B cells, which manufacture antibodies
- Even after antibodies fade away, memory T cells offer immunity against viruses
- HIV attacks T cells and gradually destroys the immune system

Treatment

Virus Busters

- The arsenal that doctors use to help fight illness
- Tackles symptoms that make people feel unwell and weak
- Uses drugs to target the causes of the problem

Feeling sick? Step back and give me some room. I can help you get well. My mission is to tackle the symptoms of a disease—the high fever, aches, and stomach trouble. Then I can start working on the cause of the disease.

I use painkillers and chemicals, such as steroids, to calm your body. I wipe out diseases caused by bacterial germs or parasitical worms using drugs such as antibiotics, which kill the invaders. But vile Virus is a tough customer. It sneaks into cells and hides. My antiviral drugs work to block Virus from copying itself, but they can't kill it, because it's not actually alive! I've made progress with HIV but have gotten nowhere with many common diseases, such as the flu. That's where Clinical Trial comes in, to show me new ways to keep you healthy.

- Steroids are natural body chemicals; doctors use artificial versions in treatments
- Broad-spectrum antivirals are new and work against several kinds of viruses
- Treatments can also include using machines to help patients breathe

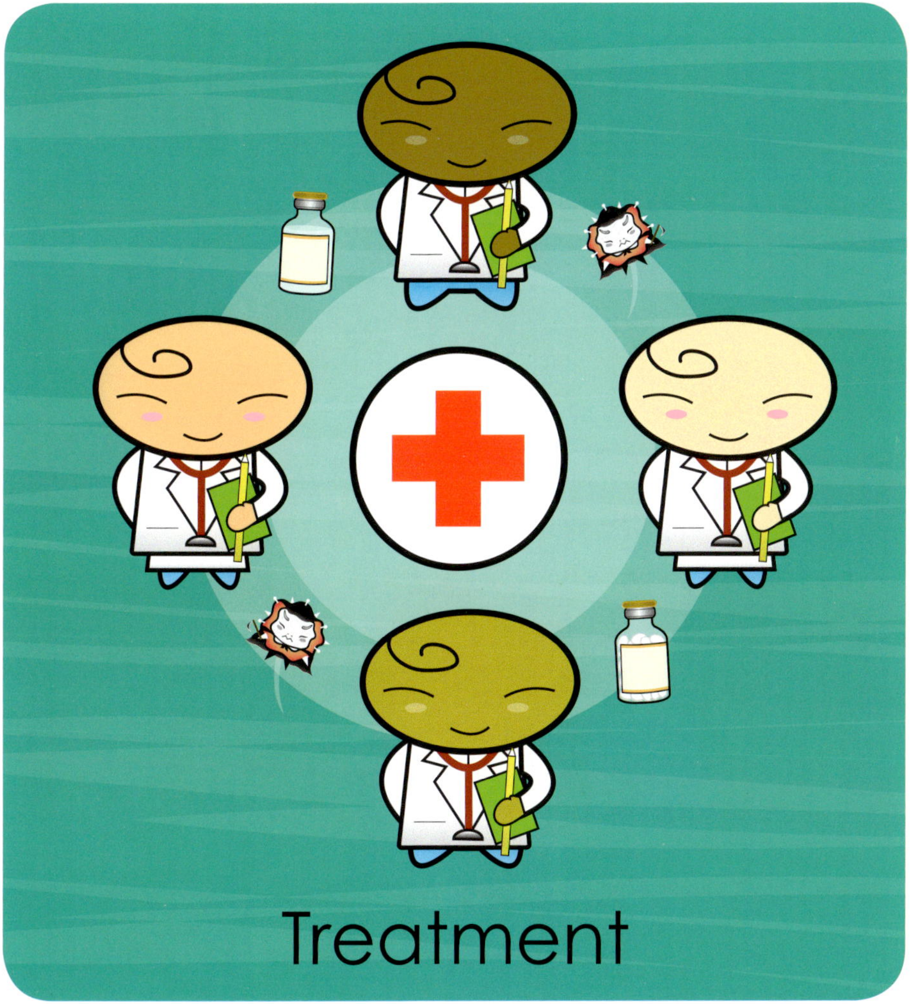
Treatment

Epidemiology

Virus Busters

- A science that goes public to track diseases
- Uses medicine, math, and detection to spot signs of danger
- Presents outbreaks as curves that it squashes with science

I'm the brains behind this virus-busting outfit, the one who sees a pandemic coming and knows what to expect. It's my job to understand how a disease spreads from person to person and ends up infecting a whole community.

I use elaborate equations to predict who will get sick, and I track victims to see how fast the disease spreads. I represent my findings as curved lines on a graph—they rise and fall as a disease comes and goes. The steeper the curve, the faster the spread. A sudden "spike" shows that an epidemic is underway, with lots of people becoming ill all at once. When that happens, I pull an action plan together to "flatten the curve," so the spread slows down to a safe level. To truly beat the disease, Vaccine, Treatment, and the Great Protectors need to help out, too.

- "Epidemiology" comes from the Greek words *epi demos*—"among the people"
- The Bills of Mortality listed how people died in London, England, in the 1600s
- Epidemiologists also find ways to help people live healthy lives

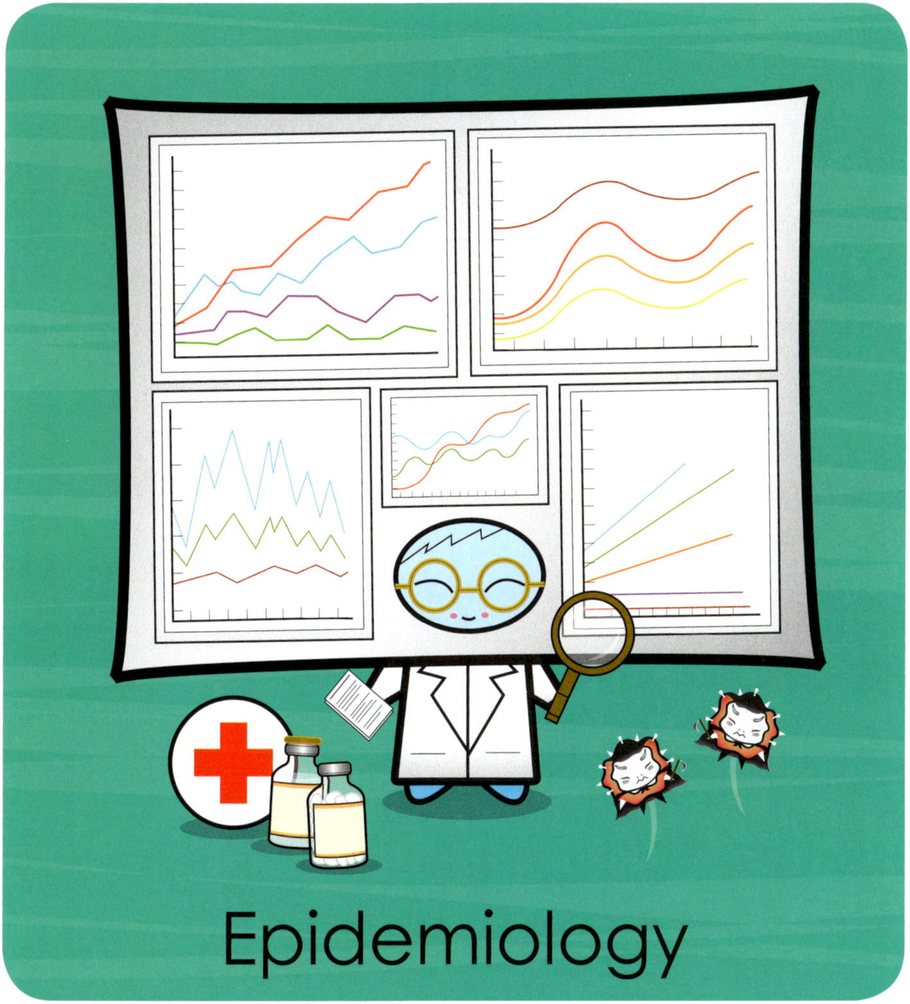

Epidemiology

Vaccine

Virus Busters

- A superhero that bestows immunity on its recipients
- Helps the immune system protect the body from disease
- Saves entire communities from diseases that kill

The silver bullet of pandemics, I'm an injection that makes the problem go away. Sure, I bring a little pain, but I also endow you with an invisible superpower. That's because, once I'm in your blood, Immune System will know enough about a disease to fight off an infection.

I teach Immune System how to make Antibody, which crushes infectious invaders from the get-go. I have a few tricks in my tool kit. Sometimes I use a weak germ or inactive Virus to wake up Immune System. Or I might just add the antigen (marker) that Antibody uses to track down infections. Once I make you immune to a disease, you can't pass it on to someone else. But be warned: unless you vaccinate everybody, a disease will eventually find its way back in, and all my skills will have gone to waste.

- The first vaccine fought smallpox (1796); it was based on a disease from cows
- Vaccination prevents about two million deaths each year
- The COVID-19 vaccination program is the largest in history

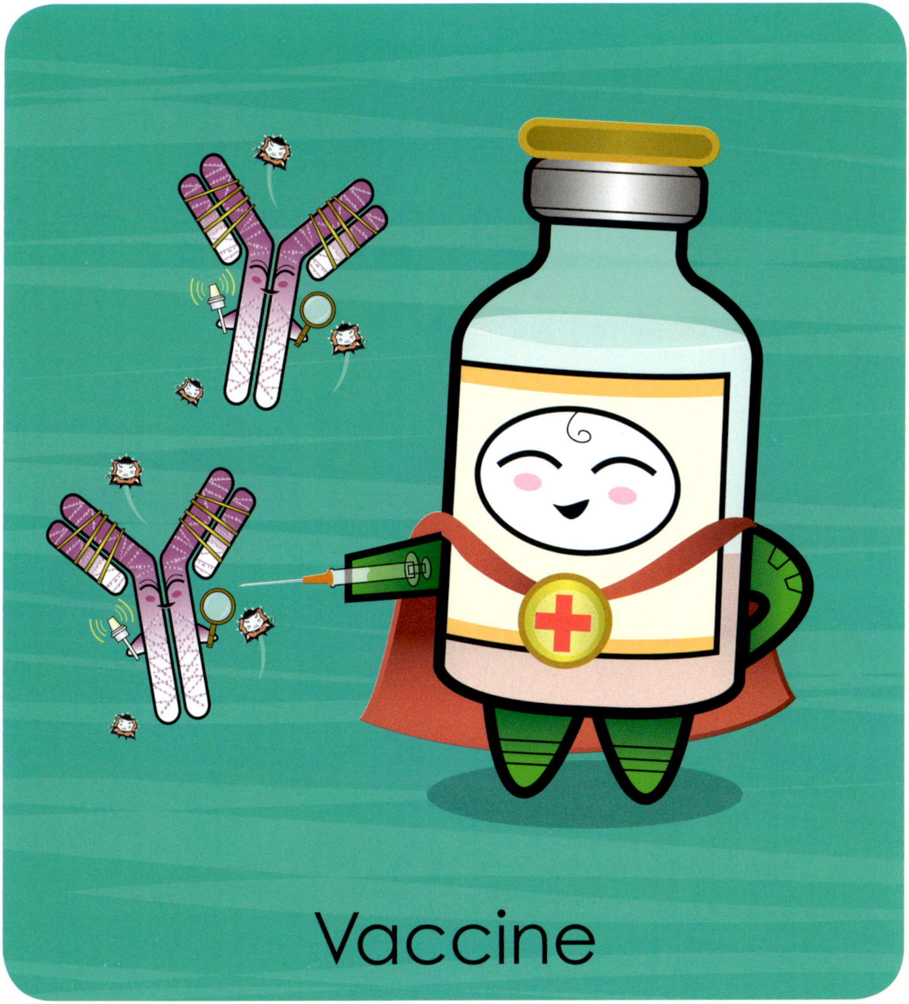

Vaccine

Clinical Trial

Virus Busters

- This safe pair of hands checks out new drugs
- Ensures that treatments do no harm
- Uses a double-blind system to avoid false results

Fighting disease is a matter of life and death, no joke. I test Treatment and Vaccine before they are used widely. Half my patients get the medicine being tested; the other half get a harmless lookalike drug (called a placebo). And my "double-blind"? Ha! No one knows which half gets which—not even the doctors. That way only the true effects of the drug are recorded.

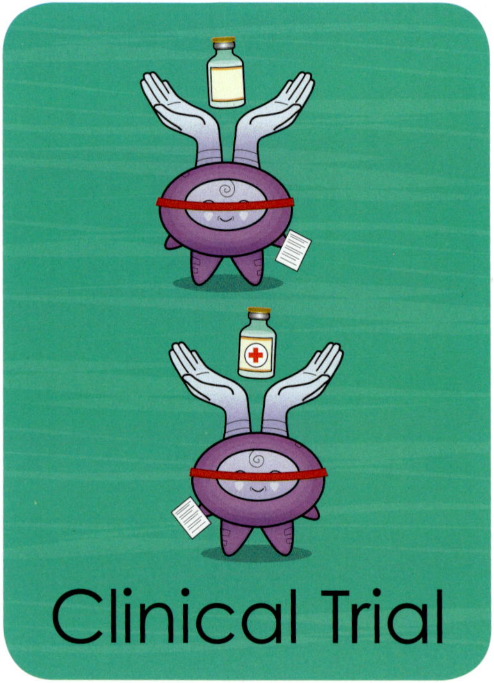

- The very first clinical trial proved that citrus fruits cured scurvy (1747)
- Modern trials use about 3,000 people to give a clear result
- Before drugs are tested on humans, they are given to other animals

Disease Modeling

Virus Busters

- Mathematical simulation of a disease's spread
- Highlights areas in which people are most at risk
- Helps figure out how to tackle a big outbreak of disease

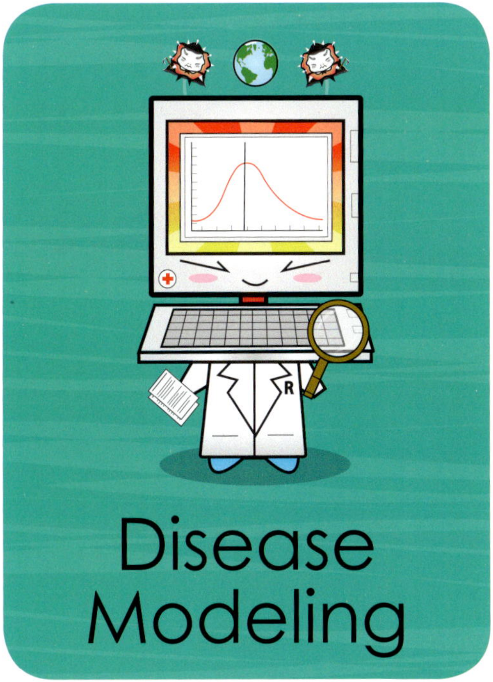

Pandemics are scary, but there is always hope with me around. You see, I give a glimpse into the future —good and bad—so you can take the right action. I calculate the chances of a disease spreading. I show how fast it will be, where it is likely to happen, and who is most at risk. I also help figure out which of the Great Protectors you should call on to help you fight a disease. Let's go!

- The earliest disease model was created in 1927
- Each model uses a reproduction (R) number
- The higher the R number, the faster the rate of new infections

New Strains

Virus Busters

- A never-ending supply of new germs
- Tiny changes that appear as a disease spreads
- May make a disease worse, but can also make it better

Virus is a real shape-shifter, changing ever so slightly as it spreads around the world. It picks up little mistakes or mutations as it makes countless copies of itself, and that's where we come in: New Strains.

This is how a pandemic can start in the first place—a new strain. No one will have seen anything like it before, so it spreads fast. But it's not always bad news, because Epidemiology and Disease Modeling use us to find out how a disease jumps from place to place. Mostly our new forms have no effect on the original disease, and sometimes they are less dangerous. It's a real plus for Virus: the less severe the symptoms, the fewer people die and so the wider Virus spreads. This is also one way in which a new disease becomes milder over time. Everybody wins!

- The COVID-19 virus was first recorded in December 2019
- One report claimed six new strains of COVID-19 were known by August 2020
- New strains of influenza virus spread around the world every year

New Strains

Chapter 3

The Great Protectors

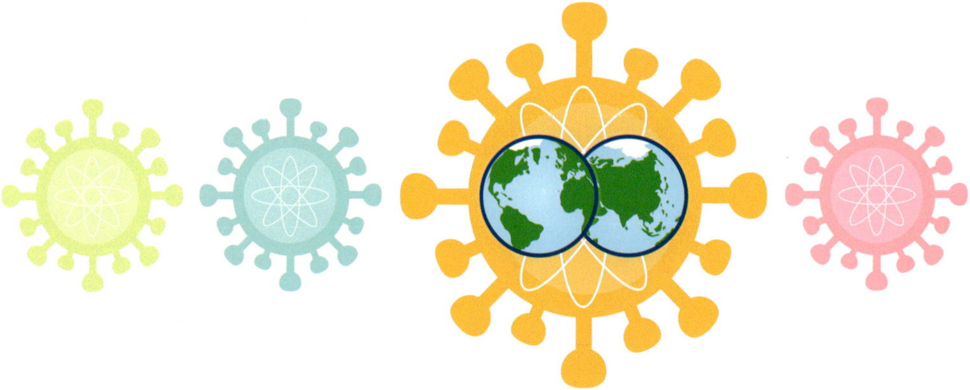

Controlling a pandemic calls for major measures, and The Great Protectors have some serious moves. At heart we are simple folk. For the most part, each of us has one important duty to perform, and we stick with it for weeks, maybe months, to get our message across. Trust in us, and no Virus will get past us—we can end any outbreak. But we big hitters are slow movers, taking tiny steps each day. Have patience, we're working, we promise. We may come and then go overnight, but you should always be ready to welcome us back. You may not like it, but stick with us. We are the top team and the best you've got.

Hygiene

Face Mask

Social Distancing

Lockdown

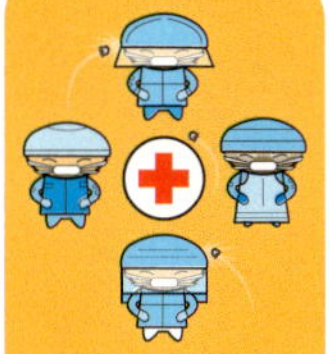

PPE

Test and Trace

Public Health Agency

Hygiene

The Great Protectors

- Flushes out dirt to fend off diseases
- Relies on clean water for food, drink, and washing
- Uses soap and warm water to get rid of nasty germs

Keep it clean, guys; that's my motto. Wash away the germs and you wash away the risk of disease. Let's look at the rules. (1) The drinking water and food you take in must be clean. (2) Anything that comes out of you must be kept well away. Wastewater is home turf for Cholera and other dirty squirts that spread in water. (3) Wash your hands whenever you get the chance. If Virus gets on your fingers, it will spread to other people with the lightest touch.

Soap and warm water will do the job. The heat damages Virus's chemicals, removing its dangerous effects, and soap dissolves the germ's fatty coat, letting water in to destroy it. Simple, no? Plus, you can stay clean on the go using alcohol gel. This spirited slop launches a chemical attack on Virus before evaporating away. Wash and go!

- One in ten people in the world do not have access to clean running water
- Every day, 1,300 children die from diarrhea caused by dirty water
- Dirty hands leave viruses on smooth surfaces, which can be infectious for days

Hygiene

Face Mask

The Great Protectors

- Stops droplets of spittle spraying virus far and wide
- Protects wearers, but also those around them
- Worn properly, it must cover the nose and mouth

I'm a nifty little protection system that catches Virus before it spreads. A piece of cloth that covers the mouth and nose, I'm here to keep you safe when there is a dangerous airborne virus out there, such as COVID-19.

I trap spit and snot drops that come out of your mouth and nose as you cough, sniff, talk, sing, and even laugh. Virus traces in these speckles of spray get stuck on me instead of spreading into the air to be breathed in by someone nearby. Sneaky Virus tends to hang around indoors, so I'm particularly effective at reducing the odds of infection inside rather than outside where there are purifying puffs of wind. OK, so I'm not fail-safe—none of the Great Protectors are—but all of us reduce the mathematical chances of Virus spreading, and that can only be good, right?

- Masks should have at least two or three layers of breathable material
- A respirator mask filters the air going in to protect the wearer
- Respirator masks don't filter the air going out, so wearers can still infect others

Face Mask

Social Distancing

The Great Protectors

- Spacing rule used when a disease starts spreading widely
- Encourages people to keep their distance from one another
- Helps reduce the airborne spread of a disease

Stand back now! You just have to give me some space. I act as a barrier to disease, and I am an effective way of choking off a pandemic virus like COVID-19, which spreads in a person's breath. Let me explain.

Your invisible bubbles of breath are filled with minuscule droplets measured in hundredths of an inch, all spreading out in front of you. Big droplets fall to the ground after about 3 feet (1 meter), but smaller droplets travel much farther. If someone has COVID-19, the droplets carry the virus. So, I draw a line for safe distancing: 6 feet (2 meters) is the absolute minimum, but please stand farther apart if you can. And no touching! I'm extreme, but I work. Along with the other Great Protectors, Face Mask and Lockdown, I can drive a pandemic out of town in a few weeks.

- If you're a child, a good measure of the gap is two times your arm span
- Coughing, sneezing, singing, and shouting can spread droplets farther
- Small droplets can linger in poorly ventilated spaces, causing infection

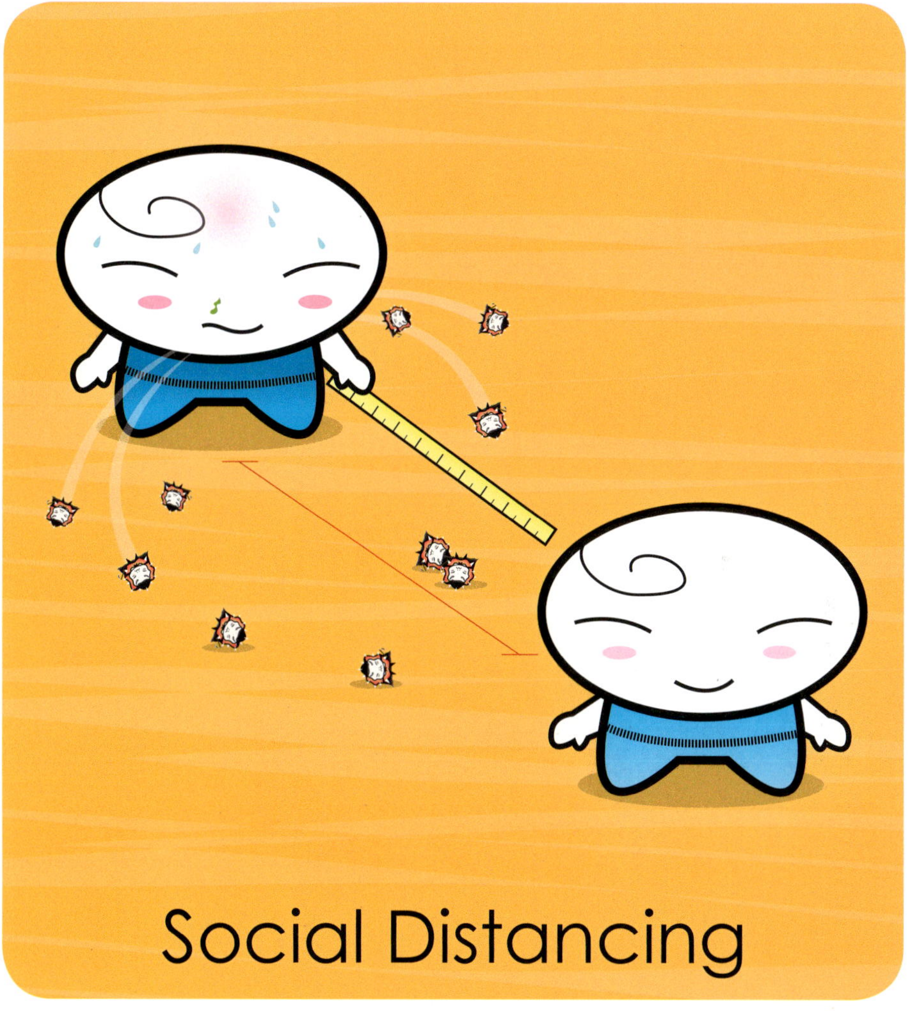
Social Distancing

Lockdown

The Great Protectors

- The biggest step used to stamp out a pandemic disease
- Blocks the spread of disease and flattens the infection curve
- This short-term lifesaver does long-term damage to jobs

An unpopular type, I'm the last resort when Virus reaches pandemic stage. I insist that you stay home to stop the spread. You see, nasty Virus needs a constant supply of new blood to fuel its need to copy itself. But with everyone at home, sufferers cannot pass on the infection. I'm all about keeping people safe and helping Epidemiology flatten its curves. Sure, if you feel well, you can go out to buy food, walk the dog, go for a jog, or ride your bike—just make sure Social Distancing tags along.

My problem is that schools and offices have to close, and people have to work from home. Many businesses struggle to survive, and the longer I go on, the more jobs I destroy. Work together to get it right, though, and Virus will have real trouble finding new victims.

- AKA "shelter in place" or a "stay at home order"
- Anyone with symptoms must not leave the house at all during lockdown
- Some countries add curfews, making it illegal to be outside at night

Lockdown

PPE

The Great Protectors

- Specialist gear worn by medical teams and caregivers
- The higher the risk of infection, the more PPE is worn
- Essential weapon in the fight against a viral pandemic

I stand for Personal Protective Equipment. I include my pal Face Mask, but I'm more readily associated with the gear worn by health professionals and caregivers who look after others during a pandemic.

Armed with masks, gloves, goggles, and gowns, I step in to keep Virus from spreading to medical staff. Sure, Face Mask does very well in a regular hospital environment, but as soon as there's a risk of infectious disease, it's on with the gloves and plastic apron, too. Should a patient test positive, out come the respirator mask, double gloves, a surgical gown, and eye protectors. I don't take any chances! Trouble is, I have a short life span—it's just too risky to clean me up for reuse. So there needs to be a lot of me around, and I mean a lot. Several billion should do it, for now. More PPE, please!

- Each hospital decides what kind of PPE should be worn in different situations
- With double gloves, the inner ones should stay infection free the whole time
- A PAPR mask uses a motorized fan to draw air into the mask for filtering

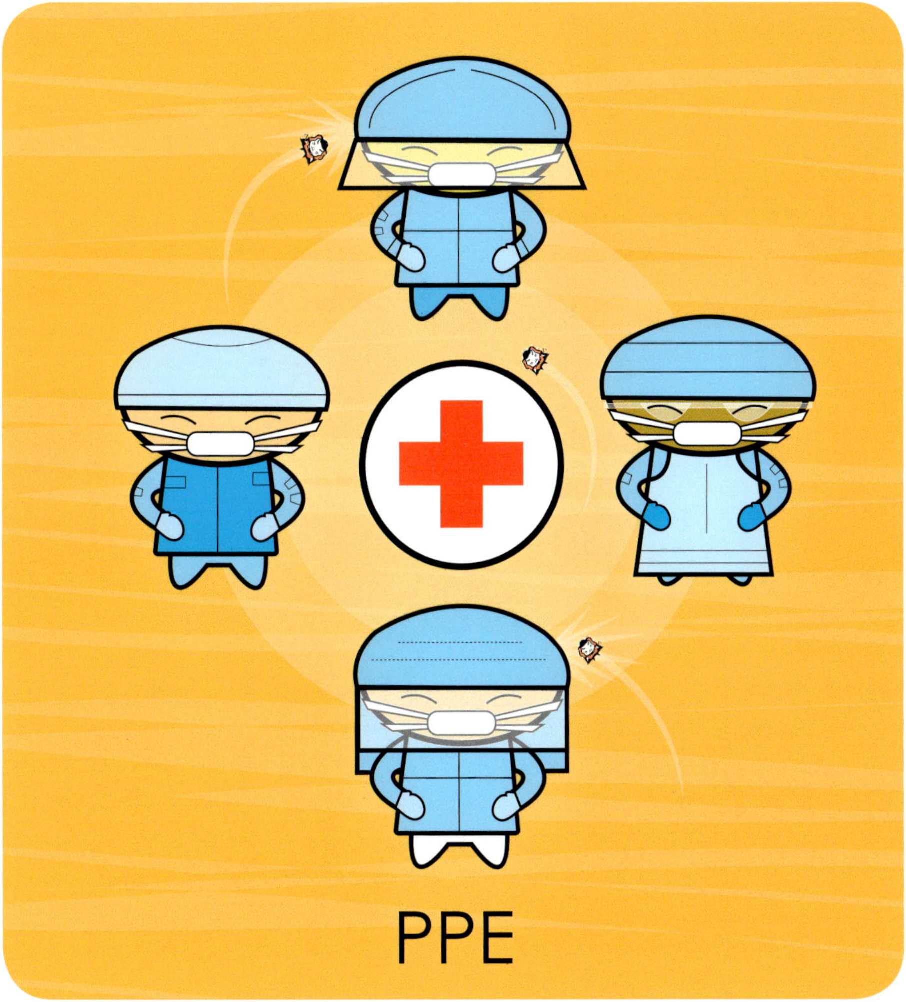
PPE

Test and Trace

The Great Protectors

- Hardworking duo that slows infections to a stop
- Testing identifies cases using high-tech RNA scanners
- Tracing tracks down the exposed and keeps them safe

Working at the sharp end of a pandemic, we're disease detectives on the lookout for people infected by Virus—and those likely to be next. Every outbreak starts with a small number of infected people in an area. The sooner we find and isolate them, the quicker we can stop an infection from spreading.

It's a huge job. First, anyone showing symptoms must isolate immediately, along with everyone they live with—they may develop symptoms, too. Test then scans for Coronavirus using a biotech kit that amplifies the bug's RNA. If the result is positive, Trace searches for close contacts of all the infected folks, asking them to quarantine (stay indoors). It's a big request, but isolating ensures that anyone who's tangled with an infected person does not become a spreader.

- If unmanaged, the reproduction (R) number of the COVID-19 virus is 3
- An R number of 3 means an infected person infects three others, on average
- Some patients are "super-spreaders," passing the virus on to dozens of people

Test and Trace

Public Health Agency

The Great Protectors

- Expert system working to make everyone healthier
- Advises on how to tackle large-scale health crises
- Calls on everyone—healthy and sick—to improve public health

Operating in every country, I busy myself with finding ways to keep a whole nation healthy. I can advise on different illnesses, on how to live more healthily, on staying safe at work or school or when traveling abroad, and more.

I'm also the one to call in a crisis—during a pandemic, for example. I consult with Epidemiology and Disease Modeling to monitor the spread of the disease. Then I send in Test and Trace to slow down the spread of the disease. If they struggle, I call on Lockdown, Social Distancing, and Face Mask to tackle Virus on a local scale. That's how I encourage the healthy to protect the weak and frail as much as they take care of themselves.

- The World Health Organization (WHO) works closely with public health agencies
- The German agency is named after Robert Koch, who linked diseases to germs
- The U.S. agency is the Centers for Disease Control and Prevention (CDC)

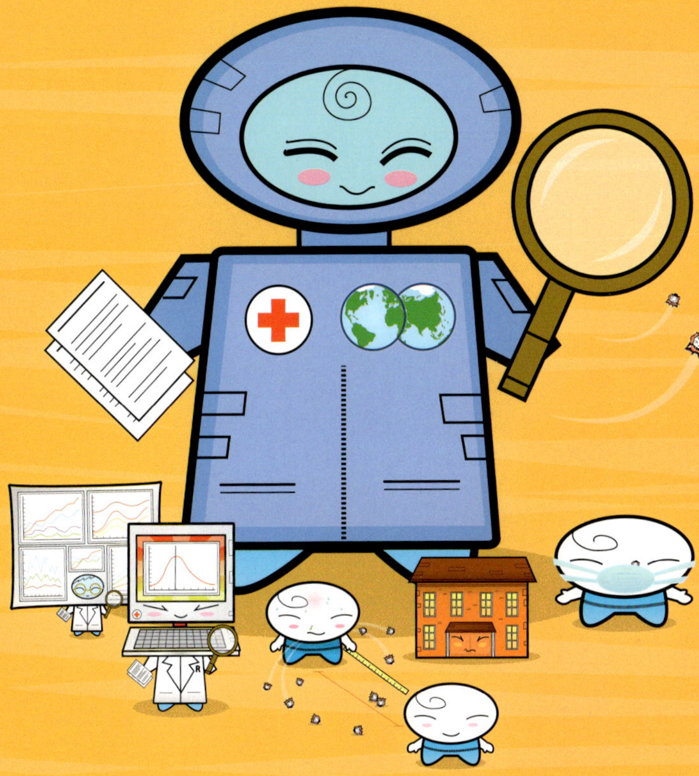

Public Health Agency

Chapter 4

Emotions "R" Us

Pandemics bring strange times. That's why the Emotions "R" Us gang gets more attention than usual. You're all locked into the same kinds of problems, sharing the same fears and frustrations. Sadness and Anxiety may take you by surprise, with Boredom blundering along behind. But while disease forces people to stay apart, it can bring everyone together, too. This is the time to let Resourcefulness step in with ideas for solving new challenges. And Community Spirit will show you that you can all work together, because you share an understanding of each other's needs.

Boredom

Anxiety

Sadness

Resourcefulness

Community Spirit

Boredom

Emotions "R" Us

- An unwelcome houseguest in a lockdown situation
- This dull demon makes things a drag
- A tough opponent in the fight for public health and safety

In a pandemic, you'll have me to fight against as well as a killer disease. Wash your hands! Wear a mask! Keep your distance! Over and over again. It's boring! Even worse is when you're stuck at home all day with Lockdown. Ugh! What can you possibly find to keep busy week after week? Of course, staying home is the right thing to do, so see if you can find ways to stick with it.

- Beat boredom by choosing an activity that has some special meaning for you
- A regular exercise routine fights boredom and keeps you fit at the same time
- In the COVID-19 pandemic of 2020, favorite authors held virtual storytimes online

Anxiety

Emotions "R" Us

- Worrisome type with a good heart but bad timing
- When worries take over and become all you can think about
- Sometimes accompanied by an instinct to play it safe

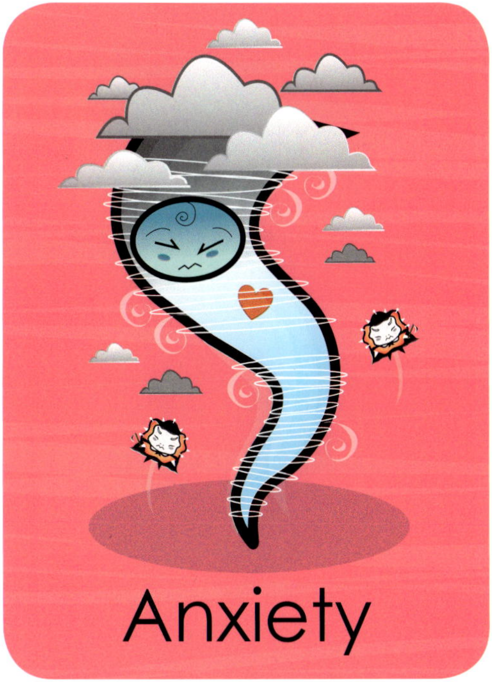

I'm a fearful character, which is not always a bad thing. Being concerned—even frightened—from time to time makes sense, right? Hard times come, and I need to watch out for them to help you keep safe. But during a pandemic, with all its unknowns, I tend to get carried away. Eek! All I can do is worry, and the more I worry the more worrisome I become. It's a real worry!

- Major causes of anxiety in a pandemic: health concerns, job loss, financial worries
- Fake news can trigger or worsen anxiety; be sure to arm yourself with the facts
- An online UNICEF story, *My Hero Is You,* explains the COVID-19 pandemic to kids

Sadness

Emotions "R" Us

- An emotion that affects everyone from time to time
- Triggered by many things, including loss and loneliness
- Can be overcome through positive action and/or support

Let's not pretend: pandemic times are sad times. They bring a good deal of suffering to many people, all at once. Community Spirit, we need you!

I feel it deep down when people get sick. Some never recover, which is devastating if they're a relative or a friend. Even healthy people struggle to stay happy all the time—*please* remember it's normal to have me in your life once in a while. I know it's lonely being stuck inside with Lockdown or forced apart by Social Distancing, and it's miserable being cut off from your friends. But these measures are all needed, so what can you do? First of all, talk to someone! You'll be amazed at the difference it can make. Then see if you can hatch a plan to switch that down-turned mouth around (even behind Face Mask!).

- People in isolation say making a plan for each day helps with loneliness
- Seek out new ways to be with friends and family online
- Help others; feeling good about yourself can lift your mood

Sadness

Resourcefulness

Emotions "R" Us

- Free-thinking radical that fits in with any situation
- Works around restrictions to keep life as normal as possible
- A team effort that fixes problems using a mix of methods

Ingenious to the core, I come to the fore in times of crisis. I feed off positive thinking to rise to the challenge when a pandemic threatens. From food-delivery services to video-chat software, I have hundreds of bright ideas for keeping things running. My plan is to keep people busy and safe, and in my world there's simply no room for Boredom and Anxiety.

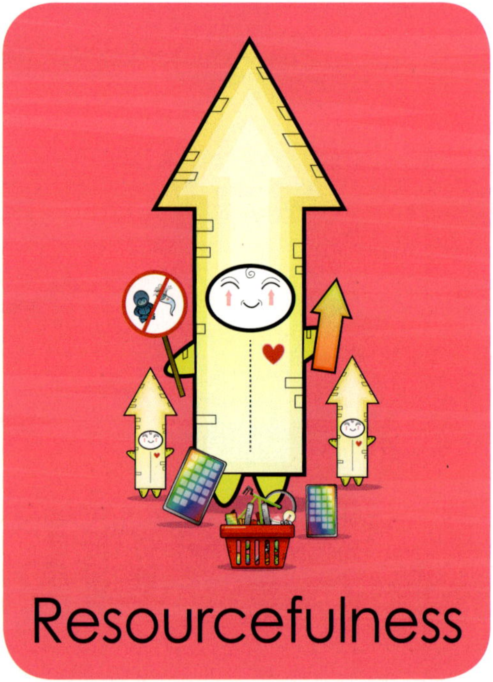

- Pandemics drive research in many areas of technology and medicine
- Isaac Newton discovered the law of gravity in lockdown against the plague
- See-through face masks allow deaf people to read lips and see facial expressions

Community Spirit

- A team player that brings people together
- A contact tracer that's on the lookout for those in need
- This helping hand holds on to all of us

Howdy! I'm a caring type who people turn to in times of trouble, such as during a pandemic. I help tackle Boredom and Sadness. My advice? Stay in touch. That way, if you need a chat, a game, or supplies, there will always be someone ready to help you out. Remember: a pandemic is an attack on all of us, so it makes sense for us to work together to stay safe. How can we lose?

- Neighborhoods connect using social media platforms and messaging apps
- The Covid-19 Mutual Aid USA website has a list of local community groups
- People who feel supported by those around them are more likely to help others

Glossary

AIDS Acquired immunodeficiency syndrome; the most advanced stage of an HIV infection when the immune system can no longer fight infections.

Antibiotics Medicine that targets bacteria but has no effect on viruses such as colds.

Antigen A chemical marker that can be used to identify an infecting virus or other germ.

Bacteria Life forms made from one single tiny cell.

Curfew A time after which everyone must stay inside their homes, usually at night.

Disease An illness where a body, or body part, is not working properly. They can range from mild to deadly dangerous.

DNA Short for deoxyribonucleic acid; DNA is a chemical that carries genetic codes that control body cells.

Epidemic When a disease becomes more common than usual in a region or country.

First responder An emergency worker who is the first person to help people in trouble; includes ambulance crew, police, and firefighters.

HIV Human immunodeficiency virus; a virus that attacks the immune system, the body's defense against diseases.

Immunity The body's ability to stop a germ from causing a disease.

Infection When a germ spreads through the body, causing a disease.

Injection When a medicine is pushed into the body through a hollow needle stuck into the skin.

Internal bleeding A very dangerous problem when blood leaks out unseen inside the body.

Isolate To stay by yourself.

Mutate To change at random.

Pandemic When an epidemic disease spreads around the whole world at the same time.

Parasite A life form that lives on or inside a larger life form.

Pneumonia A disease where the lungs stop taking in oxygen properly; it can be mild.

Protein A chemical that is essential for life; proteins are clever chemicals that work like tiny machines inside cells.

Quarantine Stopping a disease from spreading by keeping sufferers separate from everyone else.

Reproduction (R) number A number that shows how fast a disease is spreading from one person to others.

RNA Ribonucleic acid, a chemical similar to DNA that is often found in viruses.

Scurvy A disease caused by not having enough vitamin C in the diet.

Sewage Dirty waste water mixed with poop and pee.

Spittle Little blobs of spit that fly out of the mouth.

Index